PROTECTING THE PLANET FROM CLIMATE CHANGE

What's the weather like today? Some days are sunny and some are rainy. The weather over a long period of time is called climate.

The world's climate has always changed. At the moment our planet is getting hotter faster than ever before. It is mostly caused by human activities such as burning coal and oil, and cutting down forests that help keep the Earth cool.

Ice sheets are melting, oceans are getting warmer, deserts are getting larger and there are more hurricanes and tropical storms. People and animals have to find safer places to live. When one animal or plant moves or disappears from its habitat, the lives of other species that depend on it change too.

Climate change is upsetting the balance of nature and threatening the most amazing places on Earth.

But you can help and together we can protect our planet.

With thanks to:

John Sauven, Executive Director, Greenpeace UK

Dr Erika Berenguer, Senior Research Associate,
University of Oxford, Lancaster University,
Sustainable Amazon Network (RAS)

Dr Filipe Machado França, Senior Research Associate,
Lancaster Environment Centre,
Sustainable Amazon Network (RAS)

First published 2021 by Walker Books Ltd
87 Vauxhall Walk, London SE11 5HJ

2 4 6 8 10 9 7 5 3 1

Text © 2021 Catherine Barr
Illustrations © 2021 Jean Claude

This book has been typeset in Rockwell

Printed in China

British Library Cataloguing in Publication Data:
a catalogue record for this book is available from the British Library

ISBN 978-1-4063-9596-9

www.walker.co.uk

LET'S SAVE
THE AMAZON
WHY WE MUST PROTECT OUR PLANET

CATHERINE BARR   JEAN CLAUDE

WALKER BOOKS
AND SUBSIDIARIES
LONDON • BOSTON • SYDNEY • AUCKLAND

The Amazon river curves across the continent of South America before it reaches the sea. The basin of the river is filled with a vast rainforest, which is home to millions of different plants and animals. From rare orchids to rainbow-coloured macaws, tiny peanut-head bugs and sleepy sloths, this tropical paradise hosts extraordinary life.

← AMAZON

The Amazon rainforest is the biggest forest on Earth. Billions of trees form a rich green carpet that stretches across nine countries. The trees produce oxygen we breathe and soak up pollution we create. But the lush, tangled forest is disappearing fast because we are cutting down and burning so many trees. The destruction is fuelling climate change and threatening the health of the whole planet.

Let's find out why we must save the Amazon.

Let's save the Amazon

because people live there.

There are hundreds of thousands of people in the Amazon river basin, many living in towns and cities. Indigenous people live in the rainforest too, often in small, remote communities. They rely on the forest for food, shelter and medicine. River-dwelling people depend mostly on the river to survive. Cutting down the rainforest threatens everyone's way of life.

Many indigenous peoples' land is stolen from them to be turned into cattle ranches, soya fields and sugar cane plantations.

Lots of people who live in the forest travel to local towns to go to school, the market or the doctor, but some still live without any contact with the outside world.

Indigenous groups are fighting to protect their forest land with support from people around the world.

More than **30 MILLION** people speaking **195** languages live in the Amazon basin.

SAVE THE AMAZON

Let's save the Amazon

because it's a **biodiversity** bonanza.

The Amazon rainforest is noisy with invisible life. Animals hide everywhere in the thick jungle. Armies of ants march across the forest floor; jaguars slink in the shadows; monkeys swing high for ripe fruits; birds and butterflies flash in sunbeams. There may be more biodiversity – varieties of plant and animal life – in this deep forest than anywhere else on Earth.

Many plant and animal species in the Amazon are still waiting to be discovered, so it is a **TREASURE TROVE** of mystery.

Scientists know that at least **3,000** Amazon species are endangered. Their homes are threatened by new roads, mining, illegal logging and burning trees so cattle can graze.

Macaws are one of the most brightly coloured birds in the Amazon rainforest – but some are threatened because people want exotic pets.

The jaguar is a good swimmer. The secretive jungle predator often prowls the water's edge looking for a meal.

Let's save the Amazon

because its waters flow and flood with life.

The mighty Amazon river carries more water than any other river on the planet. As it flows through the rainforest endangered dolphins, red-bellied piranhas, electric eels, pancake stingrays and giant black caiman glide through its muddy waters. In the rainy season the river spills over its tree-lined banks, flooding the forest to create huge, underwater jungles.

Black caimans, endangered giant otters and jaguars that hunt from the river bank are the river's biggest predators.

No one knows why one species of Amazon river dolphin is born blue-grey, but slowly turns pale pink with age.

The number of Amazonian manatees is falling,
yet they are still hunted for their meat and skin.

Many Amazon freshwater species are endangered.
They are threatened by hunting and habitat loss.

Let's save the Amazon

because the trees SOAK UP carbon dioxide.

Human activities are adding damaging amounts of carbon dioxide gas to the air, causing our planet to get warmer. But forests naturally soak up carbon dioxide. Trees store it as carbon in their trunks, branches and roots to help them grow. The Amazon rainforest is so big that its trees take more carbon dioxide out of the air than any other forest on Earth.

Scientists call carbon dioxide a greenhouse gas because it traps heat on Earth, so the planet becomes like a greenhouse warming up in the sun.

Human activities that involve burning fossil fuels – such as driving cars, flying planes and heating our homes – release carbon dioxide into the air.

All trees take in carbon dioxide and release oxygen into the air. Life on Earth – including us – needs oxygen to breathe.

The **MAJESTIC** Brazil nut tree is really good at absorbing carbon dioxide from the air. But every tree helps in the fight against climate change.

Let's save the Amazon

because the rainforest makes rain.

All trees take up water through their roots and leaves, releasing it into the air as water vapour. Above the tree tops of the Amazon rainforest, the water vapour creates rolling blankets of clouds in the sky, called flying rivers. These clouds flow west until they meet the Andes Mountains. Then they rise and mostly blow south, bringing much-needed rain to the continent of South America.

There are around **400** billion trees in the Amazon rainforest.

Farmers in South American countries rely on rain from the Amazon's flying rivers to grow their crops.

The incredible ATTO Tower, which rises into the sky high above the forest canopy, is one of many places where scientists study climate change.

Cutting down the Amazon rainforest threatens the existence of flying rivers and the rain they bring, which in turn affects the lives of millions of people.

Let's save the Amazon
because the trees absorb the Sun's heat.

Human activities are causing the planet to become warmer, as more heat from the Sun is trapped. The dark green leaves of the Amazon rainforest soak up the Sun's heat, helping to keep the whole planet cool. When humans cut down the rainforest for farming, mining or new roads, there are fewer trees to absorb the heat of the Sun. That means that temperatures in the area, country and all around the world rise.

Cutting down the rainforest changes the weather. Water vapour from the trees creates rain so fewer trees means less rain.

Rainforest trees have shallow roots. When the soil is exposed to the sun, the roots can weaken and trees TOPPLE and fall.

Scientists measure the disappearing Amazon rainforest with lasers, drones and satellites in space.

When the forest is destroyed, the goodness in the soil quickly washes away in the rain so only poor quality soil remains.

Let's save the Amazon

because it's full of fantastic food.

Lots of familiar foods were first discovered in tropical forests. Cocoa beans that make chocolate, passion fruit and Brazil nuts all grow in the Amazon. Today thousands of different foods, including the aguaje fruit which is used in local ice cream, are harvested by people living in the rainforest. But the forested land they rely on to survive is being stolen by farmers, who bring cattle to graze, or grow animal feed for markets faraway.

Brazil and cashew nuts and cocoa beans for chocolate are rainforest friendly foods that are harvested without cutting down trees.

Clearing trees for cows, that are raised to become beef, destroys the amazing biodiversity of the rainforest.

Cattle also make climate change worse because they **FART** and **BURP** methane, a greenhouse gas.

Soya, a crop grown on cleared land, is used to feed pigs, chickens and cows thousands of miles away.

Let's save the Amazon

because it's a mystery medicine store.

Indigenous people living in the Amazon have been using plants as medicine for thousands of years. Their ancient knowledge helps their communities survive. Today many diseases from headaches to cancer are also treated with medicines that use natural ingredients from the Amazon. Yet only a tiny number of rainforest plants have so far been tested by scientists to find out if they can help cure human diseases.

Malaria is a deadly disease that can be cured with the help of quinine taken from cinchona trees in the Amazon rainforest.

The bark, flowers, leaves and roots of trees in the Amazon can be used to make medicines to treat human diseases around the world.

Amazonian people are demanding a fair share of the money made by medicine companies who discover useful forest plants.

The plant knowledge of most indigenous people is spread by word of mouth but one community has now written a huge encyclopedia about the medicinal uses of Amazon plants.

Let's save the Amazon
because life there is con

A ribbon of golden sand is carried around the world on the wind for thousands of miles from Africa to South America. Plumes of sand from the Sahara, the world's biggest desert, blow west in a stream to the Amazon, the world's biggest forest. When the dust finally falls over the Amazon basin, minerals in the sand feed the trees and plants, which helps the forest grow.

SAHARA

AMAZON

The desert dust acts as an important fertilizer for poor Amazon soils.

The special ingredient in the desert dust that helps plants grow is called phosphorous.

ected to the whole world.

Winds blow **22,000** tons (that's **250** times **HEAVIER** than one *blue whale*) of Saharan sand over the Amazon basin every year.

The flow of Saharan sand over the planet is measured by the **US** space agency **NASA**.

Let's save the Amazon

because it sounds the alarm for climate change.

Today the Amazon is on fire. Farmers are burning the forest to clear the land. They bring herds of cattle to replace the rich wildlife that once flourished there. The unique habitat is being destroyed and the huge forest is shrinking. But around the world indigenous people, communities, scientists and governments are working together, determined to save the Amazon rainforest and slow climate change.

Smoke from Amazon forest fires causes health problems for local people as well as melting glaciers high in the Andes Mountains.

Most Amazon fires are started illegally by farmers clearing land for cattle ranching.

Destruction of the Amazon rainforest affects the planet's climate and lives of people all over the world.

Right now, deforestation of the Amazon is speeding up ... but we must work together to save the biggest and one of the most extraordinary forests on Earth.

SAVE THE AMAZON

NO PLANET B

Let's save the Amazon

In the Amazon rainforest, the many trees and animals create a loud orchestra of sound. It is the biggest and one of the most amazing forests on Earth. In these pages you have found out why this huge, noisy, busy forest matters to the whole world. Now discover what you can do to help save the Amazon and protect the Earth from climate change.

Eat less meat ...

Support local meat producers who are farming alongside nature.

Try Meat-free Mondays.

Taste meat alternatives like Quorn or vegan sausages – and eat lots of vegetables, beans and lentils too!

Support Amazonian people ...

Find out about people living in
the Amazon rainforest and share
their stories by making a poster
to put up at school.

Join organizations that support indigenous groups
fighting to save the rainforest: Survival International
(www.survivalinternational.org) and Greenpeace's
Save the Amazon campaign (www.greenpeace.org).

Protect trees ...

Plant a species of tree that
belongs to the country where
you live to help soak up
carbon dioxide.

Explore your local woodland or
sit under a favourite tree to look
at the plants and animals that
depend on it to survive.

Use **100%** recycled paper and
toilet rolls sold with the FSC
logo, which helps to protect
ancient forests.